MATHEMATICS

The topics presented in this book are based on the National Curriculum requirements for Keystages 1 and 2 in Mathematics.

●

Each topic is explained fully and clearly. It is important for your child to feel happy with each explanation before embarking on the accompanying Test. You may want to check that the explanation has been correctly understood. It is a vital part of the child's development to feel that parental interest and support are present at every step. It is equally important for the child to realise that once a Test has started there is no 'outside' help until the answers have been checked by reference to pages 31 and 32.

●

All of the child's answers may be written directly into this book. Alternatively, they could be written on paper initially, together with a record of marks obtained, and a few weeks later the Tests could be taken again. This would allow an opportunity to see how the child's understanding has developed.

●

Practising Mathematics is an enjoyable and light activity. If one Test a day is undertaken, the 29 Tests will occupy almost a month, and during that time your child's understanding should deepen and mature.

Arthur Farndell

CONTENTS

Numbers	3
Adding 1	4
Adding 2	5
Adding 3	6
Subtracting 1	7
Subtracting 2	8
Subtracting 3	9
Multiplying	10
Carry-over figures	11
Long multiplication	12
Dividing	13
Remainders	14
Long division 1	15
TAKE A BREAK	16/17
Long division 2	18
Fractions, Decimals & Percentages	19/20
Adding & Subtracting Fractions	21/22
Multiplying & Dividing Fractions	23
Circles 1	24
Circles 2	25
Rectangles	26
Triangles 1	27
Triangles 2	28
Squares	29
Cubes	30
Answers	31/32

Published by
Arcturus Publishing Limited
for Index Books, Henson Way, Kettering, Northamptonshire NN16 8PX

ISBN 1-84193-045-8

This edition published 2001
Printed in Italy

© Arcturus Publishing Limited, 1-7 Shand Street, London SE1 2ES

Author: Arthur Farndell
Editor: Anne Fennell
Designer: Tania Field

NUMBERS
TEST 1

It is a wonderful fact that in Mathematics we use only **nine** figures and **zero**:

1 2 3 4 5 6 7 8 9 0

These 10 symbols make all the numbers in the universe. They can be used for counting the fingers on your hand or for telling us how many people there are in the world. In all numbers the position of each figure shows its value. You can see how the value of the figure **3** changes in this box:

THOUSANDS	HUNDREDS	TENS	UNITS	HOW TO READ THE NUMBER
			3	Three
		3	0	Thirty (three tens)
	3	0	0	Three hundred
3	0	0	0	Three thousand

Put in the right figures, with zeros where needed:

	THOUSANDS	HUNDREDS	TENS	UNITS	HOW TO READ THE NUMBER
1.			7	0	Seventy
2.				6	Six
3.	5	0	0	0	Five thousand
4.			8	0	Eight hundred

All numbers can be **POSITIVE** or **NEGATIVE**. On a warm day a thermometer shows positive numbers, but on a very cold day it registers negative numbers because the temperature is **BELOW ZERO**. To show that a number is negative we put a **subtraction** or **minus** sign before it, as in **-5**, which we call **'minus five'**.

5. Write the correct **POSITIVE** and **NEGATIVE** numbers for the dots without numbers:

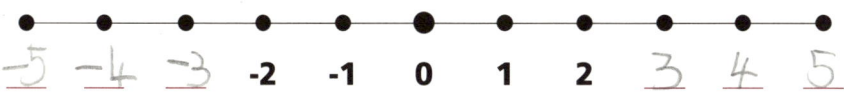

-5 -4 -3 -2 -1 0 1 2 3 4 5

Once you have learnt to read numbers, award yourself a star in the box, left.

ADDING 1
TEST 2

Grandad has to take some tablets every day. He has to take two tablets early in the morning, one tablet after lunch, and three at night time. How many tablets does Grandad take each day?

If you can add up, all you have to say is, '2 plus 1 is 3, and 3 plus 3 is 6.' So grandad takes 6 tablets every day.

Adding up is easy, even when the numbers seem to get big. Always start with the **Units** column, and then move to the **Tens**. Suppose we want to add 25 and 19. We work it out like this:

	TENS	UNITS	
	2	5	Add the Units column: 5 + 9 =14. Put the 4 in the Units answer and carry the 1 (which is 1 Ten) to the column. Now add 2 and 1 and the new 1 to obtain 4 for the Tens answer.
+	1	9	
	4	4	
	1		

Now try these by yourself:

```
1.    T    U        2.    T    U        3.    T    U
      1    4              1    7              2    8
+     1    1        +     1    5        +     1    4
  _____            _____            _____

  _____            _____            _____
```

4. Amanda has 3 red pencils, 2 blue ones, and 4 green ones. How many pencils is that? _____

5. Jimmy has 2 computer games. He is given 2 more for his birthday and 5 more for Christmas. How many does he now have altogether? _____

6. How many legs do two men and two spiders have altogether? (Remember: each spider has 8 legs!) _____

Now you have completed this page, award yourself a star in the box, right.

ADDING 2
TEST 3

Even if you are adding hundreds together, it's easy. Start with the **Units** column, move to the **Tens**, and finish with the **Hundreds**. If your total for any column is bigger than 9, remember to write the second figure in this column, but carry the first figure to the next column on the left. See if you can follow what happens when we want to add 187 to 154. Here we go!

	H	T	U
	1	8	7
+	1	5	4
	3	4	1
	1	1	

Can you see that the Units total 11? The Tens total 14, which includes the carry-over figure from the 11. And the Hundreds total 3 (1 +1+ the carry-over 1).

Try the first 5 questions in the same way. Then put on your thinking cap for some harder problems!

1. H T U
    2 5 4
  + 1 7 7
  _____

2. H T U
    3 6 8
  + 2 5 4
  _____

3. H T U
    1 0 5
  + 2 5 9
  _____

4. H T U
    4 7 3
  + 2 9 9
  _____

5. H T U
    3 4 9
  + 2 6 8
  _____

6. Joe does 20 sums in one lesson, 30 in the next lesson, and 25 in the third lesson. How many sums does Joe do altogether in the 3 lessons?

7. In 1999 Mr Jenkins picked 117 apples from his tree, and in 2000 he picked 138 apples. How many apples did he pick in the two years?

8. The Thompson family had a Summer holiday that cost £475 and a short autumn break that cost £228. What was the total cost of their two holidays?

Now you can add up in hundreds, award yourself a star in the box, left.

5

ADDING 3
TEST 4

Are we ready to go into Thousands? If you know how to deal with **Hundreds, Tens,** and **Units,** it's easy, because you simply continue in the same way. Suppose you want to add 2567 and 1708. **First, put the figures in the correct columns:**

Th	H	T	U
2	5	6	7
+ 1	7	0	8
4	2	7	5
1		1	

Add the Units, to get 15. Put the 5 in the Units answer and carry the 1 to the Tens column. Add the Tens, to get 7. Add the Hundreds, to get 12. Put the 2 in the Hundreds answer, and carry the 1 to the Thousands column, to make 4 Thousand.

Here are three questions like this, and then some more problems!

1. Th H T U
       1 1 8 6
    + 1 0 9 5

2. Th H T U
       2 7 4 4
    + 1 8 3 7

3. Th H T U
       3 9 0 8
    + 2 7 6 5

4. Tonietto sold 1028 ice cream cornets on Saturday and 1054 on Sunday. How many cornets did he sell that weekend?

5. Mrs Honiton paid £1599 for a new suite of furniture, £727 for new carpets, and £1614 for some fitted cupboards and worktops. What was her total expenditure?

6. Mr Lambert earned £1428 in January, £1297 in February, and £1985 in March. How much did he earn altogether in those 3 months?

Once you have completed this page, award yourself a star in the box, right.

SUBTRACTING 1
TEST 5

Mum leaves 5 cakes on a plate in the kitchen. When she comes back from the phone there are only 4 cakes on the plate. 1 cake has been taken away! **5 take away 1 is 4**. Taking away and subtracting are the same. So we can say, 'Subtract 1 from 5 and you get 4.' We can also use the minus sign and say, '5 - 1 is 4.' The equals sign is very useful too, because we can now write **5 - 1 = 4**.

Jenny has 8 sweets. She gives 3 away. How many does she now have?
Yes, she now has 5. To find the answer you can start with 8 and count backwards 3 steps: **8, 7, 6, 5**. Or you can start from the smaller number and count forwards to the bigger number. How many steps do you take? The answer is 5, because you go from 3 to 8 in 5 steps: **3, 4, 5, 6, 7, 8**.
She has 5 sweets remaining. So we can write **8 - 3 = 5**.

Write the missing numbers:

1. 9 - 7 = ☐   2. 8 - 5 = ☐   3. 7 - 6 = ☐

4. 6 - 4 = ☐   5. 4 - 4 = ☐   6. 9 - 5 = ☐

7. 5 - 1 = ☐   8. 7 - 0 = ☐   9. 6 - 3 = ☐

10. Charlie accidentally drops one of Mum's special teacups, and it has to be thrown away. Mum had a set of 6 teacups. How many are now left? _____

Once you have understood subtraction, award yourself a star in the box, left.

SUBTRACTING 2
TEST 6

In Class 2 there are 24 children on the register. On Monday 3 children are absent. How many are present?
Yes, **21 are present**. Did you find the answer by counting backwards 3 steps from 24? Good. We can see the 3 steps like this: **24, 23, 22, 21**. You could also count forward from 3 to 24, but you would have to take 21 steps to do this!

The third way is to put the figures in the Tens column and the Units column, like this:

T	U	
2	4	In the Units column, 4 - 3 = 1.
−	3	In the Tens column, 2 - 0 = 2.
		So the answer is 2 Tens and 1 Unit,
2	1	which is 21.

Try doing these in the same way:

1. T U
     2 6
   −   4

2. T U
     3 8
   −   7

3. T U
     4 7
   −   5

4. T U
     4 5
   − 2 2

5. T U
     5 9
   − 1 8

6. T U
     3 6
   − 2 5

7. T U
     7 2
   − 5 1

8. T U
     8 4
   − 4 2

9. Marina wants to buy a dress with a price tag of £69. The manager tells her that she needn't pay £69 because in the sale there is a reduction of £12. Marina is very happy to buy the dress. How much does she pay for it?

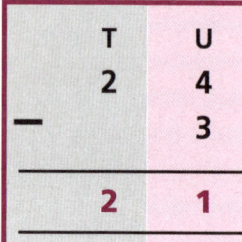

8 | When all the answers are correct, award yourself a star in the box, right.

SUBTRACTING 3
TEST 7

Putting figures into columns can be very helpful, but what do you do if the top figure in the units column is smaller than the figure under it? Let's look at this example:

	T	U
	4	6
−	1	9

Here the 6 is too small for you to take 9 away from it. So borrow 1 Ten from the top figure in the Tens column. This leaves 3 Tens. It also changes the 6 Units into 16 Units. Now you can take 9 from 16, to give 7. Finally, take 1 Ten from the remaining 3 Tens, to give 2 Tens. So the answer is 27. The full working looks like this:

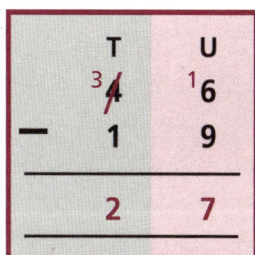

	T	U
	³4̸	¹6
−	1	9
	2	7

Follow this method carefully and you will score full marks in the test!

1. T U
    5 5
  − 2 8

2. T U
    6 7
  − 1 8

3. T U
    2 2
  −   9

4. T U
    7 1
  − 4 4

5. T U
    8 4
  − 5 5

6. T U
    6 2
  − 5 9

7. T U
    9 1
  − 7 6

8. T U
    3 4
  − 1 7

9. In the sale £15 is being knocked off a calculator that normally costs £64. What is the sale price?

10. In a special offer you can save £28 on a train ticket that normally costs £73. What is the special offer price of this ticket?

Once you have learnt to subtract, award yourself a star in the box, left.

9

MULTIPLYING
TEST 8

Suzie wants to buy 2 azalea plants. They cost £10 each. Suzie will need £20 to buy 2 plants. You can get this answer by adding £10 to £10. All you say is, '£10 + £10 = £20.'

You can also get the right answer by multiplying. This time you say, '£10 times 2 is £20.' Or you can say, '£10 x 2 = £20.'

You can see that multiplying is a way of adding numbers that are all the same. When you have only two of them, like the azalea plants at £10 each, adding is as easy as multiplying.

But if Suzie wants to buy 8 plants it is rather slow and awkward to say, '£10 + £10 + £10 + £10 + £10 + £10 + £10 + £10 = £80.' It is much easier to say,

£10 x 8 = £80

We can also set it out like this:

	T	U
	1	0
x		8
	8	0

To do these sums easily you need to know your tables by heart – all the tables from 1 to 12.
If you know them already, you will find Test 8 easy.
If you don't know your tables properly, this is a good time to practise them!
Say them aloud to a member of your family, if possible.

1. 4 x 2 = ☐
2. 3 x 3 = ☐
3. 12 x 5 = ☐
4. 6 x 3 = ☐
5. 7 x 2 = ☐
6. 3 x 4 = ☐
7. 7 x 3 = ☐
8. 9 x 2 = ☐
9. 6 x 7 = ☐

10. It costs £5 to go to the cinema. How much will it cost 4 friends altogether?

Once you have learnt to multiply, award yourself a star in the box, right.

CARRY-OVER FIGURES
TEST 9

In our work on **ADDING** we met **carry-over figures**. Do you remember? **When you get an answer above 9 in the Units column, you carry the first of the two figures over to the Tens column and leave the second figure in the Units column**.

We find the same idea of **carry-over figures** when we are multiplying. Let's take, for example, **49 x 2**. First, put the figures in the correct columns:

```
    T  U
    4  9
x      2
   ─────
    9  8
    1
```

Now multiply the 9 in the Units column by 2, to get 18. Put the 8 in the Units answer and carry the 1 to the Tens column. Now muliply 4 x 2 to get 8 and add the carried over 1 to give 9. So the answer is 98.

All of the examples are like this. Sometimes the carry-over figures are bigger than 1, but the method stays the same.

1. T U
    1 4
  x   3
  ─────

2. T U
    2 6
  x   2
  ─────

3. T U
    1 8
  x   3
  ─────

4. T U
    1 9
  x   3
  ─────

5. T U
    1 9
  x   4
  ─────

6. T U
    1 9
  x   5
  ─────

7. There are 24 pupils in Class 3. To help pay for a school outing each child brings £3 to the class teacher. How much altogether is given to the teacher?

Once you have correctly completed this page, award yourself a star in the box, left.

11

LONG MULTIPLICATION
TEST 10

Use long multiplication for numbers bigger than 12.
If you remember that there aren't in fact in fact any numbers bigger than 9, there's no problem. All you have to do is work methodically, as in all Maths. Suppose you are faced with **327 x 245**.

This means: 327 x 5 units
327 x 4 tens
327 x 2 hundreds

T/Th	Th.	H	T	U		
		3	2	7		
X		2	4	5		
	1	6	3	5	A	327 x 5 units
1	3	0	8	0	B	327 x 4 tens (write 0 in the units column)
6	5	4	0	0	C	327 x 2 hundreds (write 0 in the units and 0 in the tens column)
8	0	1	1	5		Add these 3 answers to get the grand total.

(Remember to carry the numbers over columns as you were taught in the last exercise.)

1. Th. H T U
        8 3
X   2 6
    ———————
        4 9 8
    1 6 6 0
    ———————
    2 1 5 8

2. Th. H T U
           3 7
X   1 8

3. Th. H T U
           4 5
X   2 9

4. Th. H T U
        2 1 3
X   1 2 3

5. Th. H T U
        3 0 4
X   2 1 7

6. T/Th. Th. H T U
                4 1 1
X   3 1 2

If you are an expert at multiplication, award yourself a star in the box, right.

12

DIVIDING
TEST 11

You have 6 sweets to share with your friend. **That's 3 each**, of course, because 6 divided by 2 is 3. You can write this as 6 ÷ 2 = 3.

The teacher of Class 3 wants the 24 children to walk in pairs. How many pairs will there be? Again, it is good to know the tables up to the 12 times table, because the question here is really **'How many twos in 24?'** If you remember '12 twos are 24.' then you know that **24 children make 12 pairs**. You can write this as **24 ÷ 2 = 12**. To check that you're right, you can multiply the answer (12) by the divisor (2) to get the first number (24): 12 x 2 = 24. You can see that multiplying and dividing are partners.

Here are some easy division questions. Simply write the answers:

1. 4 ÷ 2 =
2. 4 ÷ 4 =
3. 12 ÷ 4 =
4. 20 ÷ 5 =
5. 100 ÷ 10 =
6. 54 ÷ 6 =
7. 72 ÷ 9 =
8. 60 ÷ 5 =
9. 144 ÷ 12 =

10. The 24 children in Class 3 are divided equally into 4 Houses. How many children are there in each House?

11. In Class 3 the children sit 6 to a table. How many tables do they need?

12. Class 3 are going to split into 3 equal groups for a quiz competition. How many will be in each group?

Once you have correctly completed this page, award yourself a star in the box, left.

REMAINDERS
TEST 12

This time you have 7 sweets to share with your friend. As before, you can have **3 sweets each,** but now **there is one sweet left over. This sweet is called the remainder.** You can write this as **7 ÷ 2 = 3 remainder 1** A simpler way of writing this is **7 ÷ 2 = 3 r 1**

In this test all but one of the answers have remainders. See if you can find the odd one out. Write the other answers as we did with 7 ÷ 2 = 3 r 1

1. 9 ÷ 4 = ☐ 2. 17 ÷ 5 = ☐ 3. 21 ÷ 4 = ☐
4. 18 ÷ 3 = ☐ 5. 65 ÷ 8 = ☐ 6. 75 ÷ 9 = ☐
7. 146 ÷ 12 = ☐ 8. 29 ÷ 7 = ☐ 9. 23 ÷ 2 = ☐

10. Jane is planting 30 seeds. She is putting 4 seeds in each flower pot. How many flower pots does she fill?

11. How many seeds will Jane have remaining?

12. The restaurant manager seated his 60 guests at tables. 8 guests could sit at each large round table. The manager tactfully arranged for a smaller table to be brought for the guests who were 'left over'. How many guests sat at the smaller table?

Once you have learnt remainders in division, award yourself a star in the box, right.

LONG DIVISION 1
TEST 13

If you know your tables you can do a lot of dividing in your head. But if you have a big number to divide into, you can try **LONG DIVISION**.

Suppose you are asked to divide 684 by 4. Here are the steps to follow:

STEP 1
Set the numbers down like this

$$4\overline{)6\ 8\ 4}$$

STEP 2
How many fours in 6? 1, remainder 2.
Write 1 above the 6, and 2 before the 8.

$$4\overline{)6\ ^{2}8\ 4}\quad \text{(1 above)}$$

STEP 3
How many fours in 28? 7, no remainder
Write 7 above the 8.

$$4\overline{)6\ ^{2}8\ 4}\quad \text{(17 above)}$$

STEP 4
How many fours in 4? 1, no remainder
Write 1 above the 4.

$$4\overline{)6\ ^{2}8\ 4}\quad \text{(171 above)}$$

So we can now write 684 ÷ 4 = 171

Try these long division questions in the same way, following all the steps carefully.

1. $5\overline{)7\ 5\ 5}$
2. $3\overline{)4\ 8\ 9}$
3. $4\overline{)7\ 2\ 8}$

4. $2\overline{)3\ 8\ 6}$
5. $6\overline{)8\ 4\ 6}$
6. $7\overline{)9\ 8\ 7}$

7. $8\overline{)9\ 6\ 2\ 4}$
8. $3\overline{)7\ 5\ 3\ 9}$
9. $5\overline{)6\ 8\ 2\ 5}$

10. The rancher had a herd of 5684 cattle. He sold a quarter of them. How many did he sell? _____
    Tip: A quarter is one of four equal parts of a whole.

Once you have got 100 per cent, award yourself a star in the box, left.

TAKE A

GETTING THE MESSAGE

Hidden in the lines below are the letters you need to make up the Code Message.
Clue: You are searching for numbers in the 4 times table. The letters that are with these numbers make up the words. There are 3 in the first line which make up the first word, 4 in the second and 5 in the last line.

22 18 15 (40) 3 59 12 81 82 36 74
A E F   N   H P O Z T W Á   (e.g. 4 x 10 = 40)

19 90 8 59 50 31 32 41 53 20 73 45 16
E H J O L V U I J S U X T

39 29 24 18 38 44 13 57 67 4 37 46 48 66 1 6 28 9
Q Z R T H E D G M L N P A C A R X J

Code Message:

16

GOOD HEALTH, MRS JOHNSON!

Mrs Johnson is interested in buying some good wine
for a dinner party. The wine merchant is telling her
about a special offer in his store:
Today you can buy any one of these cases – that's 12 bottles
of absolutely beautiful wine – for £100.
Or you can pay 5p for the first bottle,
10p for the second bottle, 20p for the third bottle,
and so on, doubling the price for each bottle. So there you are.
The choice is yours, Mrs Johnson!

Mrs Johnson buys the wine, but she saves money
by making the right choice.
Which method of payment does she choose?

How much does she save?

LONG DIVISION 2
TEST 14

You can also use this process of **LONG DIVISION** for dividing larger numbers.

Suppose you want to divide 23 into 483.
Here are the steps:

STEP 1
Set the numbers down like this

$$23 \overline{)4\ 8\ 3}$$

STEP 2
How many time does 23 go into 4? It doesn't. Move the 4 before the 8.

$$23 \overline{)4\ ^48\ 3}\ \ ^0$$

STEP 3
How many 23s in 48? 2 r2. Write 2 above the 8 and 2 before the 3.

$$23 \overline{)4\ ^48\ ^23}\ \ ^2$$

STEP 4
How many times does 23 go into 23? 1 time exactly. Place 1 above 3.

$$23 \overline{)4\ ^48\ ^23}\ \ ^{2\ 1}$$

So we can now write 483 ÷ 23 = 21

Try these long division questions in the same way, following all the steps carefully.

1. $15 \overline{)3\ 4\ 5}$
2. $13 \overline{)2\ 9\ 9}$
3. $14 \overline{)3\ 0\ 8}$

4. $16 \overline{)3\ 6\ 8}$
5. $21 \overline{)6\ 7\ 2}$
6. $23 \overline{)7\ 1\ 3}$

Once you have conquered long division, award yourself a star in the box, right.

FRACTIONS, DECIMALS & PERCENTAGES

Fractions, **decimals** and **percentages** are not as difficult as they may seem. They are all ways of describing parts of a unit.

A **fraction** means **a fragment or small piece.** It tells us how many parts of one unit, e.g. half a biscuit, two thirds of the class.

A **decimal** shows us how many **tenths**, **hundredths** and **thousandths** of one unit.
Two examples are:

Th	H	T	U	.	Tenths	Hundreths	Thousandths
			0	.	5		
		1	5	.	2	5	

In the first example you have **no units**, but **five tenths of one unit**. This is written as **0.5** (nought point five).

*This is the same as a **half** or $\frac{1}{2}$ because **10 tenths equal one whole unit** and so 5 **tenths is a half**.*

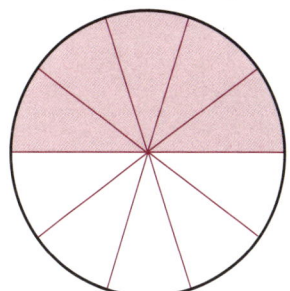

We can illustrate this in a pie chart. Here **ten pieces equal a whole unit**. We can describe the shaded part either as $\frac{5}{10}$ or **0.5** in the decimal form. Both answers show **a half of a whole**.

In the second example we have 1 ten, 5 units, 2 tenths and five hundreths. We read this as **15.25** (fifteen point two five). To illustrate this:

● ● ● ● ●   We have **15 whole parts**
● ● ● ● ●
● ● ● ● ●

2 tenths (two parts of 1 whole).

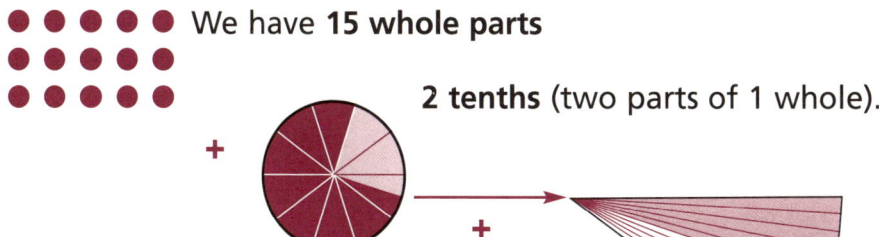

If each tenth is split into 10 we have **5 of these parts** (five hundredths).
So, a **decimal** is a way of explaining a **part of one unit** in divisions of ten.

Once you have understood these fractions, award yourself a star in the box, left.

19

FRACTIONS, DECIMALS & PERCENTAGES
TEST 15

A **percentage** tells us **how many out of 100**.
If you achieved **half marks** in an exam we show this as **50%** (50 out of 100 or fifty per cent).

$\frac{1}{2}$ **0.5**   **50%**   are the same.

To **change a fraction to a decimal**, **multiply the top number of the fraction by 10** and **divide the answer by the bottom number**. Then **divide the answer by 10** by adding a 0 and a decimal point at the beginning.

$\frac{1}{2}$ x 10 = $\frac{10}{2}$ ⟶ $2\overline{)1\,^10}$ = 5

Divide it by 10 by adding 0 and a decimal point at the beginning **= 0.5**

To **change a fraction to a percentage**, **multiply the top number of the fraction by 100** and **divide the answer by the bottom number**. Remember to add the percentage sign (%).

$\frac{1}{2}$ x 100 = $\frac{100}{2}$ ⟶ $2\overline{)1\,^10\,0}$ = **50%**

To **change a decimal to a percentage**, simply **multiply the decimal by 100** or **move the decimal point 2 places** to the right to give the correct answer.

0.5 x 100 = 50%

Show that you have understood by completing these examples. The first one is done for you.

Changing a fraction to a decimal and a percentage

For example: $\frac{1}{2}$ 0.5   50%

1. $\frac{1}{5}$ ___ ___
2. $\frac{1}{10}$ ___ ___
3. $\frac{1}{4}$ ___ ___

20

If you have correctly completed the questions, award yourself a star in the box, right.

ADDING & SUBTRACTING FRACTIONS
TEST 16

We know that a fraction has **2 numbers, one above the other**.
The top number is called the **numerator**, and the bottom number is called the **denominator**.
So in $\frac{1}{2}$ the **numerator** is **1** and the **denominator** is **2**.

When we want to add 2 fractions with the same denominator, we **simply add the 2 numerators** without changing the denominator. For example,

$$\frac{5}{11} + \frac{2}{11} = \frac{7}{11}$$

It's just the same with subtractions.

For example,

$$\frac{5}{11} - \frac{2}{11} = \frac{3}{11}$$

Try these in the same way:

1. $\frac{1}{15} + \frac{1}{15} = \square$

2. $\frac{2}{9} + \frac{5}{9} = \square$

3. $\frac{7}{11} + \frac{2}{11} = \square$

4. $\frac{4}{7} - \frac{1}{7} = \square$

5. $\frac{8}{17} - \frac{2}{17} = \square$

6. $\frac{4}{5} - \frac{1}{5} = \square$

7. $\frac{3}{17} + \frac{7}{17} = \square$

8. $\frac{11}{23} - \frac{9}{23} = \square$

Once you have completed this page, award yourself a star in the box, left.

ADDING & SUBTRACTING FRACTIONS
TEST 17

But suppose you want to add $\frac{1}{2}$ to $\frac{1}{3}$. Now you have two different **denominators**. So these are the steps to take:

1. Find the lowest number that **2 and 3 both divide into exactly**. **This is 6**. This number is called the **Lowest Common Denominator** or **LCD**

2. Take the first fraction ($\frac{1}{2}$). Divide the LCD (**6**) by the denominator (**2**) and multiply the answer by the numerator (**1**). This gives us 3 as the new numerator, and so we can express $\frac{1}{2}$ as $\frac{3}{6}$.

3. In the same way we can express the second fraction $\frac{1}{3}$ as $\frac{2}{6}$.

4. Add the new numerators **3 + 2** ($\frac{3}{6}+\frac{2}{6}$) to give the final answer: $\frac{5}{6}$

   The full expression is:

   $\frac{1}{2} + \frac{1}{3} = \frac{3}{6} + \frac{2}{6} = \frac{5}{6}$ If you want to subtract $\frac{1}{3}$ from $\frac{1}{2}$, use the same method:

   $\frac{1}{2} - \frac{1}{3} = \frac{3}{6} - \frac{2}{6} = \frac{1}{6}$.

Try these as well:

1. $\frac{1}{3} + \frac{1}{4} = \frac{\_}{12} + \frac{\_}{12} = \frac{\_}{12}$

2. $\frac{1}{4} + \frac{1}{5} = \frac{\_}{20} + \frac{\_}{20} = \frac{\_}{20}$

3. $\frac{1}{2} + \frac{1}{4} = \frac{\_}{\_} + \frac{\_}{\_} = \frac{\_}{\_}$

4. $\frac{3}{10} + \frac{2}{5} = \frac{\_}{\_} + \frac{\_}{\_} = \frac{\_}{\_}$

5. $\frac{1}{3} - \frac{1}{4} = \frac{\_}{12} - \frac{\_}{12} = \frac{\_}{12}$

6. $\frac{1}{4} - \frac{1}{5} = \frac{\_}{20} - \frac{\_}{20} = \frac{\_}{20}$

7. $\frac{4}{5} - \frac{1}{10} = \frac{\_}{\_} - \frac{\_}{\_} = \frac{\_}{\_}$

8. $\frac{1}{2} - \frac{1}{7} = \frac{\_}{\_} - \frac{\_}{\_} = \frac{\_}{\_}$

Once you can add and subtract fractions, award yourself a star in the box, right.

MULTIPLYING & DIVIDING FRACTIONS
TESTS 18, 19

When you want to multiply two fractions, **multiply the two numerators** (top numbers) and then **multiply the two denominators** (bottom numbers). It couldn't be easier.

Look at this example: $\frac{2}{3} \times \frac{1}{7} = \frac{2}{21}$

Test 18 Multiply these fractions in this simple way:

1. $\frac{3}{5} \times \frac{4}{11} = \square$ 2. $\frac{4}{7} \times \frac{5}{9} = \square$ 3. $\frac{1}{3} \times \frac{2}{5} = \square$

4. $\frac{3}{7} \times \frac{1}{2} = \square$ 5. $\frac{1}{4} \times \frac{1}{5} = \square$ 6. $\frac{1}{2} \times \frac{1}{3} = \square$

7. $\frac{1}{10} \times \frac{3}{5} = \square$ 8. $\frac{1}{9} \times \frac{2}{3} = \square$ 9. $\frac{1}{6} \times \frac{1}{11} = \square$

When you want to divide one fraction by another, simply **tip the second fraction** (the divisor) **upside down, change the division sign to a multiplication sign**, and **go ahead as if you were multiplying**. If you can follow this example, you should have no trouble scoring full marks in this next test:

$\frac{2}{5} \div \frac{1}{2} = \frac{2}{5} \times \frac{2}{1} = \frac{4}{5}$

Test 19

1. $\frac{1}{7} \div \frac{2}{9} = \frac{1}{7} \times \frac{9}{2} = \square$

2. $\frac{1}{9} \div \frac{1}{4} = \square = \square$

3. $\frac{1}{5} \div \frac{1}{2} = \square = \square$

4. $\frac{1}{3} \div \frac{2}{5} = \square = \square$

5. $\frac{2}{7} \div \frac{1}{2} = \square = \square$

6. $\frac{1}{8} \div \frac{2}{3} = \square = \square$

7. $\frac{3}{11} \div \frac{1}{3} = \square = \square$

8. $\frac{2}{7} \div \frac{3}{5} = \square = \square$

Once you have successfully completed the tests, award yourself a star in the box, left.

CIRCLES 1

A circle is a beautiful shape. It has a **CENTRE** and a **CIRCUMFERENCE**, which is the boundary line of a circle. Every point on the circumference is the same distance from the centre as all the other points.

A straight line from the centre to the circumference is called a **RADIUS**. The plural of radius is **RADII**.

A straight line going right across the circle and through the centre is called a **DIAMETER**. The diameter is twice as long as the radius. The diameter produces two angles, each of 180 degrees, which we write as **180°**.

If we take a quarter of a circle we produce a **RIGHT ANGLE**, like the corner of a table. A right angle has 90°. The large angle which remains has 270°.

If we **BISECT** a right angle (cut it in half), we have two angles, each of 45°. Each of these is an **ACUTE ANGLE** (less than 90°)

The movement all the way round the centre is **360°**. You can calculate this by **adding the four right angles** together: 90° + 90° + 90° + 90° = 360°

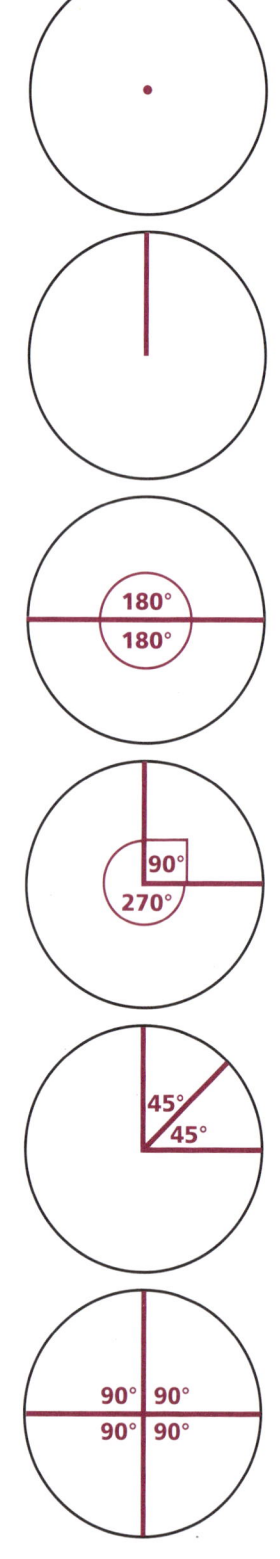

Once you have gone around in circles, award yourself a star in the box, right.

CIRCLES 2
TEST 20, 21

The large hand of a clock (the minute hand) **is like the radius of a circle**. When this minute hand goes from 12 to 3, how many degrees does it pass through?

Yes, it passes through 90°.

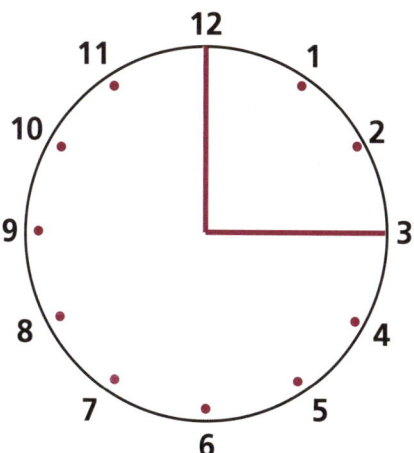

Test 20 How many degrees does the minute hand pass through when it moves from:

1. 12 to 1?
2. 12 to 2?
3. 12 to 4?
4. 12 to 6?
5. 12 to 7?
6. 12 to 9?
7. 12 to 11?
8. 12 to 12?

We know that the diameter of a circle is twice as long as the radius. If the radius is 1cm, what is the diameter? **Yes, it must be 2cm.**

Test 21 Fill in the empty boxes.

	Radius	Diameter
Example	1 cm	2 cm
1.	2cm	___
2.	2.5cm	___
3.	___	6cm
4.	___	7cm
5.	10cm	___
6.	12cm	___
7.	___	100cm
8.	___	1000cm

Once you have successfully completed these tests, award yourself a star in the box, left.

RECTANGLES
TEST 22

A rectangle has four straight sides and four right angles.

This rectangle is 5cm long and 2cm wide.

FINDING THE AREA OF A RECTANGLE
The area of a rectangle is all the space it occupies on the paper. To find the area of a rectangle is very easy.

Multiply the length by the width: 5cm x 2cm = 10cm^2.

We read this as **'ten square centimetres.'**
You can see why the area of this rectangle is ten square centimetres if you divide it into square centimetres, like this:

Write the areas of these rectangles in cm^2.

	Length	Width	Area
Example	5 cm	2 cm	10 cm^2
1.	4 cm	3 cm	_____
2.	6 cm	1 cm	_____
3.	2.5 cm	2 cm	_____
4.	3 cm	1 cm	_____
5.	5 cm	3 cm	_____
6.	7 cm	6 cm	_____
7.	1.5 cm	1 cm	_____
8.	8 cm	7 cm	_____
9.	10 cm	3.5 cm	_____
10.	12 cm	11 cm	_____

Once you have understood your areas, award yourself a star in the box, right.

TRIANGLES 1
TEST 23

On page 24 we looked at a rectangle 5cm long and 2cm wide. We calculated its area as 10cm². This means that half its area is 5cm².

Let's look at the rectangle again, but this time with a single **DIAGONAL** dividing the area into equal halves.

Each half is a **right-angled triangle**.

The **area of each triangle is 5cm²**.

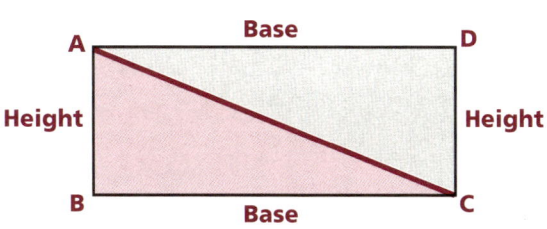

We can write:
Area of △ABC = 5cm².

We can also write:
Area of △ADC = 5cm².

We can understand why the area of a triangle is found by multiplying the base by the height and dividing the answer by 2.
So the formula for the area of a triangle is $\frac{1}{2}$ BH (**half the BASE times the HEIGHT**).

Write the areas of these triangles in cm².

	Base	Height	Area
Example	5 cm	2 cm	5 cm²
1.	4 cm	3 cm	___
2.	6 cm	1 cm	___
3.	3 cm	2 cm	___
4.	7 cm	4 cm	___
5.	2 cm	1 cm	___
6.	8 cm	5 cm	___
7.	5 cm	4 cm	___
8.	6 cm	3 cm	___
9.	10 cm	6 cm	___
10.	8 cm	2 cm	___

Once you have understood triangles fully, award yourself a star in the box, left.

TRIANGLES 2
TEST 24

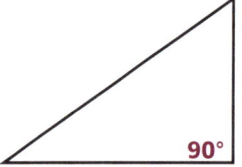

We have already met the **RIGHT-ANGLED** triangle.

An **EQUILATERAL** triangle has three equal sides and 3 equal angles

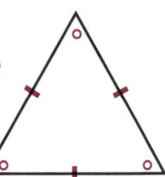

An **ISOSCELES** (say EYE-SOSS-A-LEES) triangle has two equal sides and two equal angles.

A **SCALENE** (SKAY-LEEN) triangle has no equal sides and no equal angles.

Now, an amazing fact about triangles is that the **three angles always add up to 180°**, no matter what shape the triangle is. So in an **equilateral triangle each angle is always 60°!**

If you know 2 angles, you can add them together and take the answer away from 180° to find the 3rd angle.

In this test we are told the first 2 angles of a triangle. What is the third angle?

	1st angle	2nd angle	3rd angle
Example	60°	20°	100°
1.	50°	50°	___
2.	40°	40°	___
3.	60°	40°	___
4.	55°	75°	___
5.	84°	63°	___
6.	72°	91°	___

Once you have worked out the angles, award yourself a star in the box, right.

SQUARES
TEST 25

When a **number is multiplied by itself** the answer is called the **SQUARE** of that number.

> **So the square of 2 = 2 x 2 = 4 .**

It is called a **square number** because 4 dots can show the shape of a square –

The square of 3 = 3 x 3 = 9.
Nine dots can also show the shape of a square –

All the square numbers are like this.

A simple way to write the **square of 2** is 2^2.

The **square of 3** can be written as 3^2, and so on.

We read these numbers as **'two squared,' 'three squared,'** and so on.

Write the squares of the numbers.

		Square
Example	2^2	4
Example	3^2	9
1.	4^2	_____
2.	5^2	_____
3.	6^2	_____
4.	7^2	_____
5.	8^2	_____
6.	9^2	_____
7.	10^2	_____
8.	11^2	_____
9.	12^2	_____
10.	1^2	_____

If all your answers are correct, award yourself a star in the box, left.

29

CUBES
TEST 26

A cube is the next step on from a square.

Multiply a square by the original number to find the CUBE of the number. For example,

> the cube of 2 = 4 x 2 = 8

What this shows is that the cube of 2 is really **2 x 2 x 2 = 8**.
It is called a **CUBE** because 8 dots can show the shape of a cube.

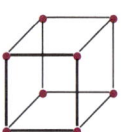

A simple way to write the **cube of 2** is **2^3**, which we can read as '**two cubed.**'

The **cube of 3** is **3 x 3 x 3 = 27**.
The cube of 3 can be written as **3^3**, which we can read as '**three cubed.**'

The cube numbers quickly become large, as we shall see in the Test.

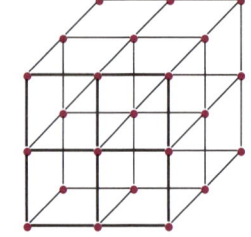

Write the cubes of the numbers.

		Cube
Example	2^3	8
Example	3^3	27
1.	4^3	_____
2.	5^3	_____
3.	6^3	_____
4.	9^3	_____
5.	10^3	_____

Once you have worked out all the cubes, award yourself a star in the box, right.

ANSWERS

TEST 1
1. 70   2. 6   3. 5000   4. 800
5. -5, -4, -3 ... 3, 4, 5,

TEST 2
1. 25   2. 32   3. 42   4. 9   5. 9
6. 20

TEST 3
1. 431   2. 622   3. 364   4. 772
5. 617   6. 75   7. 255   8. £703

TEST 4
1. 2281   2. 4581   3. 6673   4. 2082
5. £3940   6. £4710

TEST 5
1. 2   2. 3   3. 1   4. 2   5. 0   6. 4
7. 4   8. 7   9. 3   10. 5

TEST 6
1. 22   2. 31   3. 42   4. 23   5. 41
6. 11   7. 21   8. 42   9. £57

TEST 7
1. 27   2. 49   3. 13   4. 27   5. 29
6. 3   7. 15   8. 17   9. £49   10. £45

TEST 8
1. 8   2. 9   3. 60   4. 18   5. 14
6. 12   7. 21   8. 18   9. 42   10. £20

TEST 9
1. 42   2. 52   3. 54   4. 57   5. 76
6. 95   7. £72

TEST 10
2. 666   3. 1305   4. 26199   5. 65968
6. 128232

TEST 11
1. 2   2. 1   3. 3   4. 4   5. 10
6. 9   7. 8   8. 12   9. 12   10. 6
11. 4   12. 8

TEST 12
1. 2r1   2. 3r2   3. 5r1   4. 6
5. 8r1   6. 8r3   7. 12r2   8. 4r1
9. 11r1   10. 7   11. 2   12. 4

TEST 13
1. 151   2. 163   3. 182   4. 193
5. 141   6. 141   7. 1203   8. 2513
9. 1365   10. 1421

TAKE A BREAK
The code message is:
NOW JUST RELAX.

Mrs Johnson decides to pay £100.
She saves £104.75

TEST 14
1. 23   2. 23   3. 22   4. 23   5. 32
6. 31

TEST 15
1. 0.2, 20%   2. 0.1, 10%
2. 0.25, 25%

TEST 16
1. $\frac{2}{15}$ 2. $\frac{7}{9}$ 3. $\frac{9}{11}$ 4. $\frac{3}{7}$ 5. $\frac{6}{17}$
6. $\frac{3}{5}$ 7. $\frac{10}{17}$ 8. $\frac{2}{23}$

TEST 17
1. $\frac{4}{12} + \frac{3}{12} = \frac{7}{12}$
2. $\frac{5}{20} + \frac{4}{20} = \frac{9}{20}$
3. $\frac{2}{4} + \frac{1}{4} = \frac{3}{4}$
4. $\frac{3}{10} + \frac{4}{10} = \frac{7}{10}$
5. $\frac{4}{12} - \frac{3}{12} = \frac{1}{12}$
6. $\frac{5}{20} - \frac{4}{20} = \frac{1}{20}$
7. $\frac{8}{10} - \frac{1}{10} = \frac{7}{10}$
8. $\frac{7}{14} - \frac{2}{14} = \frac{5}{14}$

TEST 18
1. $\frac{12}{55}$ 2. $\frac{20}{63}$ 3. $\frac{2}{15}$ 4. $\frac{3}{14}$ 5. $\frac{1}{20}$
6. $\frac{1}{6}$ 7. $\frac{3}{50}$ 8. $\frac{2}{27}$ 9. $\frac{1}{66}$

ANSWERS

TEST 19
1. $\frac{9}{14}$ 2. $\frac{1}{9} \times \frac{4}{1} = \frac{4}{9}$
3. $\frac{1}{5} \times \frac{2}{1} = \frac{2}{5}$
4. $\frac{1}{3} \times \frac{5}{2} = \frac{5}{6}$
5. $\frac{2}{7} \times \frac{2}{1} = \frac{4}{7}$
6. $\frac{1}{8} \times \frac{3}{2} = \frac{3}{16}$
7. $\frac{3}{11} \times \frac{3}{1} = \frac{9}{11}$
8. $\frac{2}{7} \times \frac{5}{3} = \frac{10}{21}$

TEST 20
1. 30° 2. 60° 3. 120° 4. 180°
5. 210° 6. 270° 7. 330° 8. 360°

TEST 21
1. 4cm 2. 5cm 3. 3cm 4. 3.5cm
5. 20cm 6. 24cm 7. 50cm
8. 500cm

TEST 22
1. 12cm^2 2. 6cm^2 3. 5cm^2
4. 3cm^2 5. 15cm^2 6. 42cm^2
7. 1.5cm^2 8. 56cm^2 9. 35cm^2
10. 132cm^2

TEST 23
1. 6cm^2 2. 3cm^2 3. 3cm^2
4. 14cm^2 5. 1cm^2 6. 20cm^2
7. 10cm^2 8. 9cm^2 9. 30cm^2
10. 8cm^2

TEST 24
1. 80° 2. 100° 3. 80° 4. 50°
5. 33° 6. 17°

TEST 25
1. 16 2. 25 3. 36 4. 49 5. 64
6. 81 7. 100 8. 121 9. 144
10. 1

TEST 26
1. 64 2. 125 3. 216 4. 729
5. 1000